Ignite Your Success

Your LifePlan Revolution

Gerald Duran

GERALD|DURAN

www.geraldduran.com

GERALD|DURAN

ISBN (Print): 978-0998544823
ISBN (eBook): 978-0-9985448-3-0

DEDICATION

This workbook is dedicated to all the risk-takers who chase their dreams.

CONTENTS

INTRODUCTION

Deep inside every one of us is a dream — the American dream. A desire to do something remarkable with our lives. Something that matters.

Have you ever felt as if you were born to do something greater than anything you are presently doing?

Fact is, 70 percent of U.S. workers loathe their jobs. They only keep doing them to pay the bills. Millions more Americans are without jobs. According to the Associated Press, 53 percent of recent college graduates are jobless or underemployed.

With all this bad news, we have lost our ability to dream beyond our present circumstances. Because we feel "stuck," we have erected invisible barriers (excuses) that block the path to what's actually possible. As a result, we are only dreaming about one inch from our present circumstances.

We are searching for meaningful careers and purposeful lives. In this book, I will help you find the ingredients you're still missing to pursue the dream still living deep inside you. I will help you identify the right path to reaching your destiny.

Ask yourself this question: What would you set out to accomplish if you had all the resources and knew you COULD NOT fail?

You see, most of us struggle to define what will make us happy: is it the American dream, the ideal career, a relationship, a new house, a great car, or a certain income? We want to know what will make us happy and how we will know when we "get there."

When life has not worked out the way we planned, it's natural to wonder why we are on this planet and whether this is all there is. There must be more!

I firmly believe that deep inside each of us is a God-planted dream, and that our pursuit of that dream, the journey to our destiny, is the way we will find true fulfillment. This truth, which I learned from one of my mentors, has radically changed everything for me. I believe it can change everything for you too!

"Your future is not determined by your present circumstances. Your future is determined by God's plan and purpose for your life, the size of your dreams, and your perception of what's possible!"

-1-
SCORECARD

WHAT would change in your life if you had a dream job with a dream income? How would your lifestyle change? Would you live in the same place, drive the same car, pay off your debts, save or invest more, have more freedom to "...."? What would change?

WHY spend our entire careers, about one-hundred thousand hours, in jobs that are never going to get us where we need to go? The size of our paychecks determines where we live, where we shop, what we can buy, where our kids go to school, and whether we'll be able to retire someday or resort to handing out carts at Wal-Mart instead. No offense intended if that's what you really want to do after you've put in your one-hundred thousand hours, but my point is our incomes determine way too much of our lives to ignore the drivers that control their size, and ultimately our destiny.

And money is but one slice of the pie. Enjoying what we do, making a difference, having purpose, and doing something meaningful are only some of the desires that most of us have in life.

But before we respond to the what and the why of what I just said, we need to examine our present results by being brutally honest about what got us here. UNLESS we can accept complete responsibility, despite our challenges, set-backs, and failures, we are only victims who are unable to change our future. We have bought into the lie that our circumstances determine where we will "end up."

So let's examine your results thus far. Let's check your scorecard.

If you play a sport, your scorecard tells the world what kind of player you are. You may think you're a great golfer, but your scorecard begs to differ. If you're a business owner, your profit and loss (P&L) tells the world how successful your business is.

Your company may seem successful to you: A hundred people work for you, you have fancy offices, you pay yourself a large salary, but at the end of the day, if your scorecard says you're losing your rear, your scorecard is the truth. No matter what you say, it does not lie.

If you have a career, your paycheck, your salary, is your career scorecard. It does not have to be big; it just has to get you where you are going. And if it doesn't, what are you going to do about it?

To change your results, you have to be willing to change your thinking. Your BEST thinking has gotten you to where you are. How you think controls what you do. What you do controls your results. Think. Do. Results. This is your scorecard.

You see, the moment you awaken to the fact that if you can perceive it, you can do it ... that thinking changes everything. That thinking says "My future is not determined by my present circumstances. It's determined by God's plan and purpose for my life, the size of my dreams and my perception of what's possible." That's a revelation that will change everything about your journey and your results.

We fail for lack of knowledge. We simply don't know how. The difference between the person making two hundred thousand a year and the person making thirty thousand a year is the person earning two hundred thousand knows how. If the person making thirty thousand knew how, he or she would be making the two hundred thousand.

If you could have, you would have, but you didn't, and your scorecard proves it. If you desire to change, then you are willing to learn. You are ready to learn to change your way of thinking so you can change your way of doing and change your results.

Ok, so how do you change your destiny? The first thing you do is GET ONE! Get a destiny, a destination. Reignite your dreams. Ignite your success.

Gerald Duran

NOTES

Gerald Duran

-2-
DREAM JOB. DREAM INCOME.

What is success? Every person has a personal definition of what it is, and that's the way it should be. The definition of success is what most people believe will make them happy. For most of us, part of that equation is a dream job with a dream income. And for those who aren't interested in getting paid well enough to reach their goals and dreams, that's what fast-food jobs are for. After all, someone needs to make our tacos … it's all yours.

Okay, let's assume that success is for you after all.

Imagine a dream job with a dream income. Wow! Who wouldn't want that? Doing something you are great at, something you enjoy, and something that provides you with the financial provision to fuel your dreams. This is what eludes most of us at every job.

I have asked the following question to thousands of individuals I've met in career interviews over the years, and I am still surprised at how many people answer it the same way: "So if you worked for me and were doing an excellent job (I mean everything that you touched turned to gold), how much would I be paying you in five years?" Then I ask "in two years?" And then "in twelve months?" I like to see if they've thought this through, if they actually have a plan. Some of the common responses I get are:

"Well, I'd have to see the job description."
Code for: "I allow others to determine my value."

"Money isn't everything; I'm not trying to be a millionaire."
As if they were on the brink of becoming one!

"Oh, I've never thought about that."
Meaning: "I failed to plan, so I plan to fail."

Baloney. You alone should determine how much you need to make. And you should know how much you need to make every year to accomplish your goals. As a result, you must find an employer or client willing to pay that much. We need to forecast our future income requirements in the same way every successful business does.

So what does it take to land that dream job with a dream income? The two required ingredients are:

1.   A Success Mindset
2.   A Relevant Skillset

In chapters three through five we will dissect the Success Mindset. In this chapter, we will explore the Relevant Skillset. Every marketplace has in-demand skills it is looking for. And if you have these in-demand skills, it's pretty easy to get hired and paid well.

In-demand doesn't necessarily equate to well paid, however. The home care workforce, for example, some 2.5 million strong, is one of the nation's fastest-growing <u>yet also worst paid.</u>

As always, supply and demand define relevancy, meaning in-demand and high-paying are the keys. If, for instance, you are a software developer, aka coder, companies are willing to pay generously for your skills because the demand is huge, growing, and coupled with a shortage of individuals who have the most sought-after skills.

Another hot career is the modern entrepreneur. Demand has emerged for a new type of entrepreneur who must be a technologist, business model innovator, lead generation strategist, and creative director with the know-how to engage prospects and customers through emerging technologies. As is always the case, the tools and strategies that were cutting-edge just a few years ago are becoming obsolete.

If your present skill-set has grown obsolete or just doesn't pay well, it's time to begin exploring and trading in your old skill-set for an in-demand and high-paying one. And don't make the same mistake that so many others are making in going back to college. It's not going to help you a get a relevant skill-set. That'll just compound the problem by putting you deeper in debt.

If you wanted to explore a hot career like software development or the modern entrepreneur, for example, look for coder or entrepreneurial bootcamps. That's where the industry will send you to reskill, someplace where you'll leave with real skills the market will pay for. They're not cheap but they are a much better investment than another college degree because you'll end up ahead for both time and money.

Resist automatically ruling out the unfamiliar jobs like a software developer, modern entrepreneur, or something else outside your comfort zone. People often say, "Oh, I don't think I'd like doing that." The fact is, they don't really know. That's like saying, "Oh, I don't think I'd like being a millionaire." But if you are not earning enough to fuel your dream, ultimately you won't like what you do no matter what. Look for in-demand and high-paying careers. Then explore how you can develop the relevant skill-set needed to land a dream job with a dream income. Expect to learn something new, make sacrifices, and take smart risks.

While you will risk much in choosing the narrow path of pursuing your personal dream, you will suffer great regret if you don't ... the pain of not becoming who you thought you were destined to be.

Gerald Duran

NOTES

Gerald Duran

-3-
IGNITE YOUR DREAM

Remember when we were young? Boy, could we dream. Anything and everything was possible. We could become the President of the United States, a superhero, a mogul, a celebrity, or a professional athlete. There were no barriers and nothing was off limits. If we could dream it, we could do it!

As time has rolled along we've allowed our perception of what's possible to shrink. Sadly many of our dreams remain buried under a mountain of caution, doubt, and fear. The big dream now seems too risky and quite unrealistic. I mean, where would we even start? It is only a thought of an earlier time, the foolishness of a fantasy, perhaps the same fantasy we get from purchasing a lotto ticket. We might hope or dream, but we don't believe.

Ask yourself this question: What would you set out to accomplish if you had all the resources and knew you could not fail?

You see, most people struggle to define what will make them happy — the American dream, the ideal career, a relationship, a certain house, a specific car, or a certain level of income. People want to know "What will make me happy, and how will I know when I get there?"

When life has not worked out the way we planned, it's natural to ask,

"Why am I on the planet? Is this all there is? There must be more."

So why would you purposely spend one hundred thousand hours of your life in a job doing unfulfilling tasks just to pay the bills? No one would do that on purpose, right? But that's often the very result of living life without purpose.

If you are reading this book, congratulations! You are a small and unique part of the worker population who has decided not to settle for whatever life serves you. Life is hard. It's full of up's and down's. So to have hope for the future, you need a destination. And that's where the dream comes in.

Did you know that your ability to dream is based upon your perception of what's possible? **Your perception frames your future and your results.** Your goals are based on what you believe is possible and this drives your decisions and results. Your ability to believe in your dreams is extremely powerful. Perception frames your results.

Reset Your Perception

Set aside a relaxing weekend morning with your favorite cup of coffee, and visualize or paint a portrait of your dream lifestyle.

Example:

I see myself living in a cottage home near the waterfront with a beautiful front porch and manicured landscaping. In my driveway is a vintage Jaguar convertible that I've restored. In the back yard is a pool of cool water next to my outdoor living space. I see my kids playing in the pool and my wife entertaining our friends while I'm grilling up the steaks. Our home is paid for; we have no debt; we are happy. What a wonderful life ....

Now ask yourself, "Can I see myself in this dream? Does it seem possible?" Can you perceive yourself living the life?

Caution! Never dream on a budget. Can you imagine an artist who could only paint what he thought he could afford? How limiting.

People tend to struggle with this dreaming-on-a-budget idea. We have to bust through the natural tendency to dream about one inch from our present circumstances. The typical excuse is, "Well I'm just being realistic." But why would you limit your future to your past-limited experiences? So give yourself a break and have fun with the dreaming exercise. Add up the cost *after* you have dreamed the perfect lifestyle, not *while* you're dreaming it.

So what are the costs associated with your dream? How much time will you spend planning it, how much money will it cost you, how much energy will you put into it, and how much are you willing to sacrifice to get it?

Most people do not have a LifePlan. They're just winging it. We've all heard the adage, "fail to plan, plan to fail." The question becomes which side of the population do you want to be on, the side that determines your own future, or the side that accepts life as it is?

Now back to the dream cottage. Complete the dream vocationally. What type of dream career will result in that dream lifestyle? **Happy dreaming!**

As you begin to explore the possibilities with a dream lifestyle, this next step is critical to moving forward. It's what separates the wannabes from the doers. We've all met people who have gigantic, and sometimes ridiculous, dreams. So what makes a dream ridiculous? It's not the size of the dream. It's one's failure to commit a vision to writing.

Wannabes never move on to this next step.

What separates the posers from the achievers is the people who get things done invest the time to write them down. Sounds simple, right? But when you dream beyond your present circumstances, it's often hard to write things down. If you are stuck in a lousy job, deep in debt, living month to month, writing down your dream feels silly ... unbelievable even.

Maybe you've just graduated college with a degree in marketing and you're just starting your career. Congratulations! Yet after months of trying to land an actual marketing job, you find yourself working at the mall and back home living with the folks. Depressing. It's hard to have faith in yourself or your dream. Faith is seeing what is not as though it were. **Write down your dream.**

Dream It. Do it.

Write it down. Then dream some more. Edit your dream and change it some more. Have fun with this. Get together with a friend or significant other to discuss the possibilities. There will always be reasons and excuses why you can't do something; focus on the reasons why you can.

As you begin to commit your dreams to writing, your perception of what's possible will begin to change. Your goals will change. **Your decisions will change. Your actions will change. And then your results will change.**

Your dream will serve as a mental picture of your dream lifestyle and destiny, what you are working toward.

The next step is to vision-map a LifePlan. First, itemize and prioritize the areas in life that are important to you. Then write down your dream, goals, and action steps for each area of importance.

1.   **Prioritize – Important areas of my life.**
2.   **Dream – My dream for each area of priority.**
3.   **Goals – My goals for each area of priority.**
4.   **Steps – Steps to each area of priority.**

This is called a **LifePlan:** deciding where you want to go, your destination, then deciding when you want to get there and which choices you'll need to make to get there.

Prioritize: Itemize the areas of your life in order of importance to you.

Example:
1.   My Faith
2.   My Mental & Physical Health
3.   My Marriage
4.   My Family
5.   My Career
6.   My Finances

Dream: Write down your dream for each area of importance.

Example:

Area 1: I see myself confident in my faith.
Area 2: I see myself as healthy, in shape, with a fresh image.

Goals – Write down your goals for each area.

Example:

In order to reach my dreams and goals, I will make a list of the top three careers that meet my personal criteria. Then I will explore where I can get the right education and skills to get hired.

NOTES

Gerald Duran

-4-
THE CONTINUOUS LEARNER

Have you ever met an outperformer — someone who seems to surpass his or her peers in terms of success and sustainability? This person can experience failures, setbacks, and whatever else life seems to throw his or her way, but this person will always bounce back, each time a little stronger than before.

Outperformers are like Timex watches; they can take a licking and keep on ticking. They are very different than one-trick ponies who have one gig that flops and never seem to bounce back. Outperformers have a mentality that understands if you want ongoing success, you'll need nine lives ... or seasons. Why? Because life is full of seasons, and every season eventually comes to an end. They understand the landscape is always changing, so they either have to change with it or get left behind. They don't just survive; they thrive. It's a mentality ... a way of thinking.

So what's their secret? **Outperformers are continuous learners.**

Continuous learners adapt and reinvent. They stay relevant by learning new things. They don't waste their time trying to fix symptoms; instead they focus on solutions to problems. They know if they want to change something important in their lives, they have to be willing to grow. And to grow they have to be willing to learn.

Learn > Grow > Change

If, for instance, you need to earn $127,000 a year to reach your goals, but you earn only $67,000 a year, the reason you don't make the $127,000 is because you don't know how. I mean if you knew how, you'd do it, right?

Your Problem: Lack of Knowledge
Your Symptom: Lack of Money

The continuous learner would do whatever was required to gain the knowledge to earn more. Continuous learners are comfortable in their own skin. They are humble, grateful, and confident. To them, lack of knowledge is an opportunity to grow. They don't make excuses, blame their circumstances, their clients, their employers, or the economy. While these might be actual challenges, continuous learners refuse to be the victims of circumstances.

Think about all the companies that failed to learn and reinvent and got left behind as a result. Blockbuster Video is probably the blockbuster of great examples. They had the largest slice of the pie and the resources to dominate. They could hire the smartest people, pay for the top technologies, and yet they got left behind. Why? They failed to reinvent. They had a profound lack of knowledge about the impact of the digital revolution. And worse, they had pride and ego issues. They didn't have a learning heart.

The opposite of the learning heart is the stubborn heart. Those who have a stubborn heart have all the excuses and reasons to fail. Nothing's never their fault. Pride and ego hold them back. They focus on all the reasons why something can't be done. They are angry and defend their failures instead of learning from them.

Successful people who have reached the proverbial mountaintop realize they are standing on mountains of mistakes converted into success. They are continuous learners who have gained the know-how to succeed.

NOTES

Gerald Duran

-5-

MASTER LIFE'S UPS AND DOWNS

Life is full up's and down's. It's a journey where you're likely to encounter much adversity, a place where mountains block the path to your destiny. At times you will be confused, lose your bearings, and feel like quitting. At times like this you must control your thought life if you want to succeed. Why? Because your thought life will control your feelings about everything in your life. Feelings are unreliable and subject to change. I've learned not to let them in my personal cockpit. Like terrorists, they have a way of hijacking things, and before I know it, I'm off course or worse, in a nose dive.

There's a battle going on in most of our minds. The battle of our thought life. The battle between doubt and faith. The battle between **I WILL SUCCEED** and **WHAT IF I FAIL?**

If we begin to entertain thoughts of doubt, our minds can progress to full-blown failure in no time flat. All of us have thoughts of doubt. But when one of those doubt thoughts enters our minds, we have to decide what we are going to do about it. If we entertain that thought, it will always progress into full-blown fear. Fear is an acronym for False Evidence Appearing Real. When we fear, it's as though we are producing, directing, and starring in our own downfall-of-me horror flick. We begin to imagine the worst possible outcomes. Fear quickly progresses into worry where we are now replaying the mental images over and over. Go figure that we are quickly stressed out — FROZEN! And then worry has its way with us and we progress into discouragement, which is operating without courage. Discouragement then progresses to depression, and depression right into failure. Our thoughts become self-fulfilling prophecies.

Doubt > Fear > Worry > Discouragement > Depression > Failure

So how do we battle doubt? We need faith. Faith is believing in our success despite our thoughts, feelings, or circumstances. When thoughts of doubt enter my mind, I've learned to call them out for what they are — TRAITORS AND TERRORISTS! Seeds of failure that I refuse to nurture. In fact, the moment I recognize them, I expose them as not my thoughts and then eradicate them from my thinking. I've learned to recognize thoughts of doubt even when they are undercover masquerading as "concerns." Same thing!

You have to be able to call what is not as though it were. All success-minded people have this ability. We've all heard the phrase, "attitude is everything." Well, if we really believed it, wouldn't we all have great attitudes? Doubters miss out on the fact that our altitude gets determined by our attitude.

Attitude is a matter of focus. It's what we allow to percolate in our minds regardless of our circumstances, failures, or setbacks. We might get a little delayed, but we are never denied. Great faith will progress to expectation, a place where we expect to win despite our circumstances. And when we experience expectation, we'll have peace ... ZERO STRESS! This peace will progress to desire, the desire to keep moving forward through all the mess. And desire progresses to perseverance, which means we'll hold onto our dreams no matter what, just like a pit-bull holds onto whatever it sinks its teeth into. It is that kind of perseverance that leads to success.

Faith > Expectation > Peace > Desire > Perseverance > Success

Winning the battle between faith and doubt is what sets apart the success-minded from the victims. How can you build your faith? Through the diligence of having a vision and a written plan, becoming a continuous learner, and investing time into developing yourself. Seek out mentors who have the battle scars from their journey, and learn from their mistakes. **Be open to reinventing you.**

NOTES

Gerald Duran

ABOUT THE AUTHOR

Gerald Duran is an INC 500 Serial Entrepreneur, CEO, Author, and Business Acceleration Mentor. For several decades, Gerald has helped CEOs and business professionals develop and reach their goals. He connects the dots between dreams, purpose, success and faith.

Gerald is the Founder and CEO of RPM Strategic, a business acceleration and venture capital consultancy; CanaMKE, an entrepreneurial accelerator; and the author of two books, HisPlan MyPlan and Ignite Your Success.

Gerald's passion is helping CEO's of small to medium-sized technology enterprises accelerate revenue through modern marketing automation and revenue performance management strategies. Gerald has 30 years of both executive leadership and consulting roles in the Coder Bootcamp and Tech-B2B sectors. His penchant for technology and actionable data drive his focus and results.

Prior to founding RPM Strategic in 2002, for 13 years Gerald was Founder and CEO to four tech ventures in the staffing, education and lead generation sectors. Gerald's leadership has landed his ventures multiple times on the prestigious INC 500, Deloitte Technology Fast 50, and Kansas City Corporate 100.

www.geraldduran.com

GERALD|DURAN

Made in the USA
San Bernardino, CA
19 April 2017